# Cambridge Little Steps 1

## Activity Book
Gabriela Zapiain

# Cambridge Little Steps 1

# ① What can we see at school?

👆 Point. 💬 Say. ✏️ Color.

**Key Language:** *teacher, boy, girl, school.* Children point to and name each item: *teacher, boy, girl, school.* Then they color the picture.

3

 **Say.** ◯ **Circle.** ✏ **Color.**

# What Can You See?

**Key Language:** *What can you see? I can see a ... teacher, boy, girl, school, sun, tree.* Children look at the story scenes. Ask: *What can you see?* Elicit answers using *I can see a (teacher).* Then ask: *Can you see a (teacher)?* Children circle and then color the items in the pictures.

# 🗩 Say. ○ Circle. ✏ Color.

Key Language: What can you see? I can see a ... teacher, boy, girl, school, sun, tree. Children look at the story scenes. Ask: What can you see? Elicit answers using I can see a (girl). Then ask: Can you see a (girl)? Children circle and then color the items in the pictures. Finally, children retell the story in their own words. Provide language as needed.

 Look. 💬 Say. ✏️ Color.

**Key Language:** *Where does the decide story take place? In a ...* Ask: *Where does the story take place?* Elicit answers and rephrase: *Yes, in a school.* Children color the picture that shows where the story takes place *(school)*.

# 👁 Look. 💬 Say. ✏️ Color.

**Key Language:** *Keep our classroom clean, children, cleaning*. Look at the scene and ask children questions such as: *Where are the children? (A classroom.) What are they doing? (Cleaning the classroom.)* Discuss why it's important to keep our classroom clean. Children color the children who are keeping the classroom clean.

**7**

👆 **Point.** 💬 **Say.** ✏️ **Color.**

**Key Language:** *book, crayon, table, chair.* Children point to and name each object: *book, crayon, table, chair.* Then they color the pictures.

 Trace. ✏ Color. 🗨 Say.

**Key Language:** *Is it a (book)? Yes, it is. No, it isn't. What is it? It's a (book).* Children look at the pictures. Ask several questions such as: *Is it a chair? Is it a crayon? Is it a boy?* Encourage children to answer with *Yes, it is* or *No, it isn't.* Children trace the school objects by following the dotted lines. Then they color the objects. Finally, they answer the question: *What is it? (It's a book.)*

9

# 📖 Match. 👆 Point. 💬 Say.

**Key Language: *open, closed, The (book) is open / closed.*** Children look at the items and draw lines to match the open and closed pairs. Then they point to each object and describe it: *The (book) is open. The (book) is closed.*

👆 **Point.** ✏️ **Color.** 💬 **Say.**

**Key Language:** *Mom, Dad, Mia, Leo, Tickles.* Point to each character and ask: *Who's this?* Children point along with you as you name the characters. Then they color the characters. Finally, children point to each character and say the name.

11

 Color. Draw. Say.

**Key Language: *What's your name? My name is ... What's his / her name? His / her name is ...*** Point to Leo and Mia and ask in turn: *What's his / her name?* Children answer and color the characters. Then point to the head and explain that children should draw hair and color it to make the character look like themselves. As they work, ask each child: *What's your name?* and encourage them to answer: *My name is ...*

 **Point.** ✏ **Color.** 💬 **Say.**

**Key Language:** *Hello. Hi!* **Goodbye.** *Bye-bye!* Children point to the pictures and decide whether the characters are saying *Hello* or *Goodbye* to each other. Then they color the pictures.
Finally, children also say *Hello!* and *Goodbye!* to each other and mime the actions. Remind them they can say *Hi or Bye-bye* as alternatives.

👁 Look. ⭕ Circle. ✏️ Color.

**Key Language:** *classroom rules, Listen. Take turns. Share.* Children look at the pictures. They draw a circle around the ones that show class rules and color them. Discuss the class rules while they are coloring, inviting children to point as you name them: *Listen. Take turns. Share.*

⊙ **Trace.** ◼ **Say.** ₁2₃ **Count.**

**Key Language: one, Show me (one). How many (books) can you see?** Children trace the number 1 several times with different colored crayons as they repeat: *One, one, one.* Then ask about the pictures in turn: *How many (books) can you see?* Children answer: *One. One (book).* They trace the number one each time.

15

 **Draw.** **Say.**

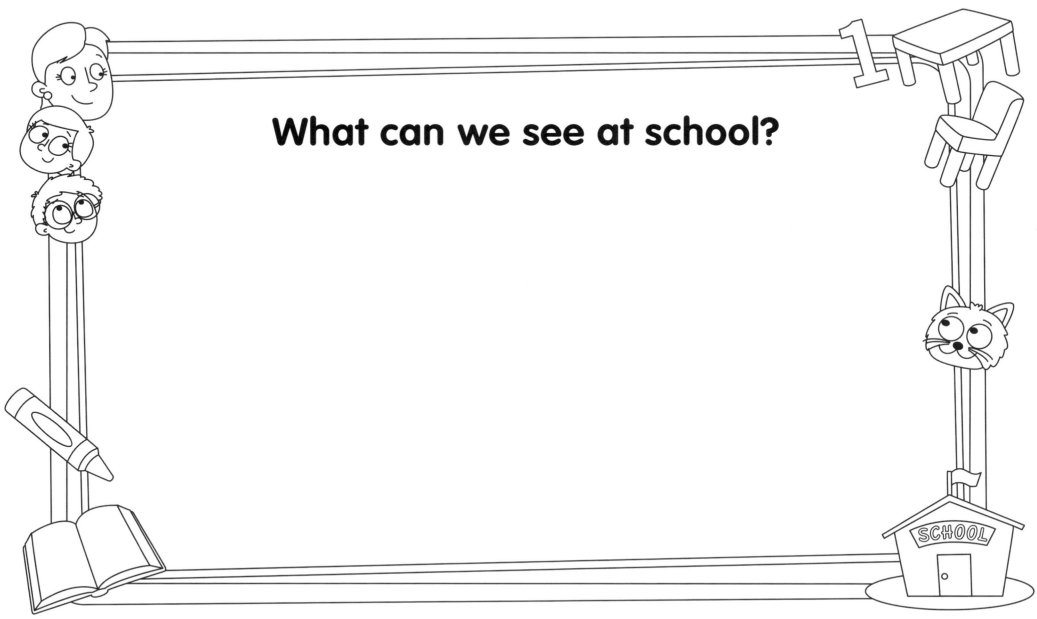

# What can we see at school?

**Key Language:** *teacher, boy, girl, school, book, chair, table, crayon, Mom, Dad, Mia, Leo, Tickles, What can you see? I can see a (girl). Is it a (table)? Yes, it is. No, it isn't. It's a (book). How many (books) can you see?* Ask the Big Question: *What can we see at school?* Children look back through Unit 1 of the Student's Book to recall what they have learned. Then they draw their favorite things from Unit 1 inside the frame. Ask volunteers to show their drawings to the class and name what they drew. Finally, answer the Big Question together, using the children's drawings to help.

## 2 What do we look like?

Trace. Say. Color.

**Key Language: *face, hair, eyes, nose.*** Children trace the lines of the key concepts: *hair, face, eyes, nose* as they name the features. Then they color the picture. Finally, children point to and name each feature again: *face, hair, eyes, nose.*

🔲 **Say.** ⭕ **Circle.** ✏️ **Color.**

# Can You Find Me?

**Key Language: *What can you see? Can you see a ...? Can you find a ...? Where is the ...?, kite.*** Children look at the story scenes. Ask: *What can you see?* Elicit answers using *I can see a ...* Then ask: *Can you see a kite?* Repeat the question using the new structures *Can you find a kite?* and *Where is the kite?* Children circle and color the kite in the picture.

# 🗨 Say. ○ Circle. ✏ Color.

**Key Language: *Can you find him / her? Where is s/he? His hair is (brown). Hair, face, eyes, hair, nose, hat, kite, mouse, character.*** Children look at the story scenes. Ask: *What can you see?* Elicit answers using *I can see a ...* Then ask: *Can you see a hat? Can you see a mouse?* Repeat the questions using the new structures *Can you find a (hat)?* and *Where is the (mouse)?* Children circle and color the items in the picture. Finally, children retell the story in their own words. Provide language as needed.

**🔲 Say. ⭕ Circle. ✏️ Color.**

**Key Language:** *character, Who are the characters in the story?* Ask children if they can remember the people or the characters in the story. Ask: *Who are the characters in the story?* Children circle and color the characters.

# 👁 Look. ✏ Color.

**Key Language: *They are different. They have the same / different hair / eyes.*** Children look at each set of pictures. In each set, they color the two children who are alike (wearing / not wearing glasses, long / short hair, girls / boys, etc.). Discuss how the children are the same and how they are different. Remind children that we are all different and that makes us all special!

 Say. Trace. Color.

**Key Language: *forehead, mouth, ears, cheeks.*** Children point to and name the following facial features: *forehead, mouth, ears, cheeks.* Then they trace the dotted lines. Finally, children color the picture.

# 👁 Look. 🗨 Say. ✏ Draw.

**Key Language:** ***This is my (nose). These are my (eyes).*** Children look at the pictures and name the missing facial features: *eyes, mouth, nose, ears*. Then they draw the missing facial features. Finally, children point to the features one at a time, name them, and point to the corresponding features on their own face and say: *This is my (mouth). These are my (eyes).*

 Point. ✏ Color. 💬 Say.

**Key Language: *red, His (hair) is red. What color is his (hair)?*** Distribute crayons. Say: *Point to the hair. His hair is red.* Children color his hair red. Repeat with *nose*. When they are finished coloring, ask: *What color is his hair / nose?*

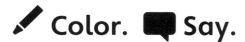 Color. 🗨 Say.

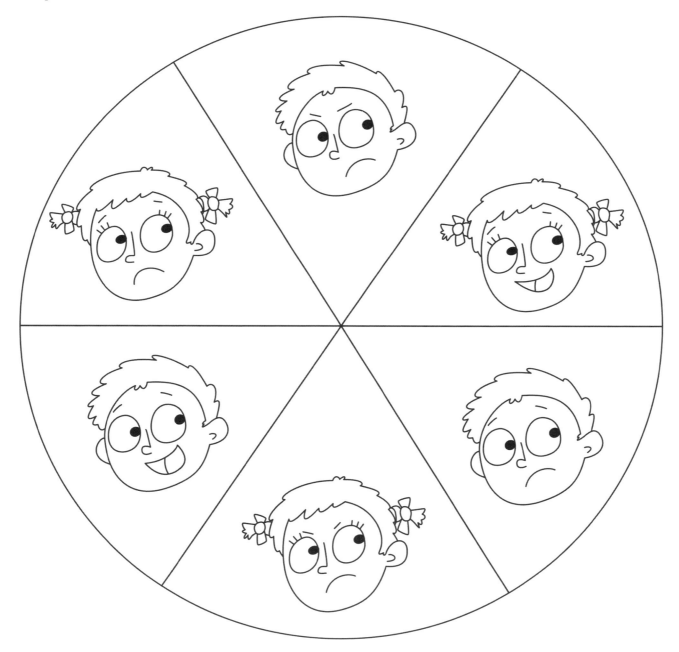

**Key Language:** *happy, sad, angry.* Children color the characters. When they're finished, take one crayon and demonstrate how to place it on the page, flat end in the center of the circle, pointed end pointing out. Then show children how to spin the crayon on top of the circle. Point to the section where the crayon is pointing, and ask: *How does he/she feel? (happy, sad, angry).* Once they understand the game, allow children to play in pairs or small groups, spinning and naming the feelings.

**25**

 Say. Trace. Color.

**Key Language:** *How do you feel? Are you happy / sad / angry? Yes, I am. No, I'm not. Is s/he sad? Yes, s/he is. No, s/he isn't.* Point to Mia and ask: *How does she feel? (Happy.)* Repeat with the remaining characters. Then children trace the mouths and color the pictures. Ensure they are tracing left to right. When they're finished, point to each character and ask different questions *(Is she sad? Is he angry?)* to elicit different answers: *Yes, she is. No, he isn't.*

# ⭕ Trace. ✏️ Draw. 🗨️ Say.

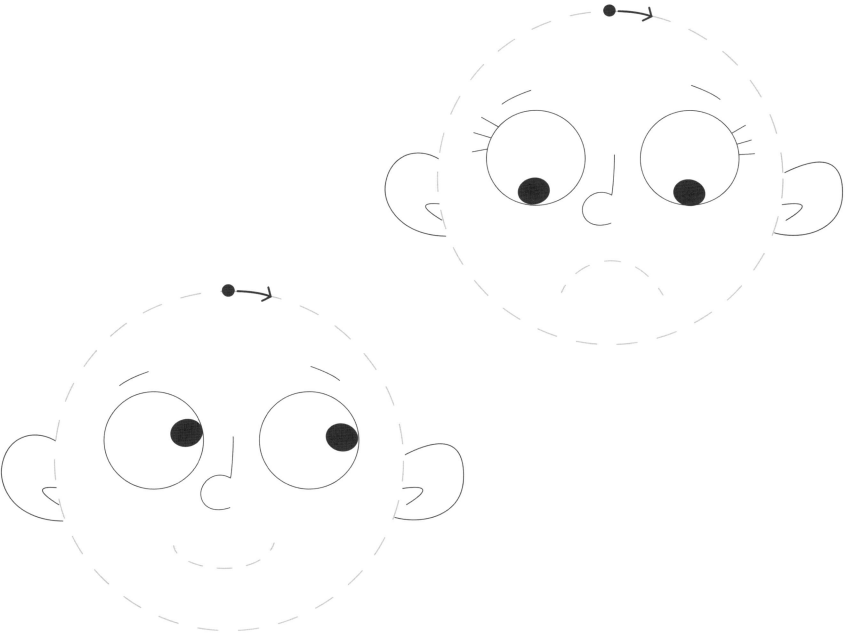

**Key Language: *How do you feel? I feel happy / sad.*** Point to each face and say *Happy or sad?* eliciting the answers. Children trace the faces and the mouths. Ask them to draw hair and color the faces to look like themselves. You can use yarn or paint for the hair if you like. As they're working, go around pointing to the faces and asking: *How do you feel? (I feel happy / sad.)*

**27**

# 👁 Look. 💬 Say. ✏ Color.

**Key Language:** *twins, They look the same / different. Do they look the same / different?* Say: *Look at the children.* Point to the first pair and say: *Do they look the same or different? What's different? What's the same?* Repeat with the second pair. Ask if both sets of children can be twins. Remind them some twins look the same and some look different. Children color the identical twins to look the same (hair, color, etc.) and the other twins to look different.

🔲 Say.  ⬭ Trace.  ¹²₃ Count.

**Key Language:** *one, two, Show me (two). How many (eyes) can you see? Let's count.* Children say the *Number 2* chant as they show two fingers: *Two, two, show me two. Show me two like this.* Then they trace the number 2. Ask: *How many eyes can you see? Let's count: One, two.* Finally, children count a partner's two eyes and two ears as they repeat: *one, two, one, two.*

**29**

 Draw. Say.

# What do we look like?

**Key Language:** *This is my hair / face / mouth / nose / forehead. These are my (eyes / ears / cheeks). This is my (nose). These are my (eyes). My hair is (brown). My eyes are (blue). I feel (happy). S/he feels (sad). Do they look the same / different? We are different.* Ask the Big Question: *What do we look like?* Children look back through Unit 2 of the Student's Book to recall what they have learned. Then they draw their favorite things from Unit 2 inside the frame. Ask volunteers to show their drawings to the class and name what they drew. Finally, answer the Big Question together, using the children's drawings to help.

# 3 What can our bodies do?

👁 Look. 🗨 Say. 📖 Match.

**Key Language: *arms, hands, legs, feet.*** Children look at and name the shaded body parts: *arms, hands, legs, feet.* Then demonstrate how to draw lines to match the pictures of the children in the top row with the corresponding body parts in the bottom row. Finally, finger trace each line, repeating the name of the body part as you link the pictures (e.g. arms – arms).

 Say. ✏ Color. ◯ Circle.

# The Coconut Band

**Key Language: *What can you see? Can you see ...? gorilla, arms, legs, hands, feet.*** Children look at the story scenes. Ask: *What can you see?* Elicit answers using *I can see ...* Then ask: *Can you see a (gorilla)? Can you see (feet)?* Children circle and then color the items in the pictures.

🗨 **Say.** ✏ **Color.** ◯ **Circle.**

THE COCONUT BAND

**Key Language:** *What can you see? Can you see ...? What can s/he / they do? gorilla, jump, arms, legs, hands, feet.* Children look at the story scenes. Ask: *What can you see?* Then ask: *Can you see (hands)?* Children circle and color the items in the picture. Then they retell the story in their own words. Provide language as needed.

# 👁 Look. ⃝ Circle. 🗨 Say.

THE COCONUT BAND

**Key Language:** *What can you see? Who are the characters? Is this from the story? What's different?* Ask children to think about the story. Ask the questions: *What is the story about? Who are the characters?* Then point to different items in the picture and ask: *What can you see? Is this from the story?* Children circle items that are not from the story (bear, guitar). Once the items have been identified, ask children: *What's different?* and discuss the differences together.

# 🗨 Say. ✏ Draw. ✒ Color.

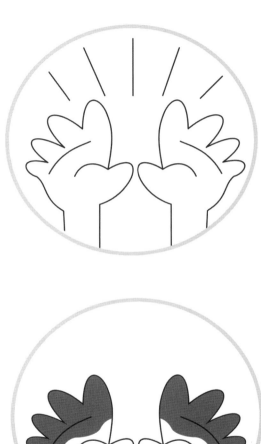

**Key Language: *Wash your hands. Soap, clean / dirty hands.*** Children look at the picture of the girl and describe what they see. Ask: *What is she doing? (washing hands)*. Then point to the two pictures on the right and ask: *What can you see? (Clean hands, dirty hands)*. Ask again: *Does the girl have clean hands or dirty hands?* Elicit the answer *clean hands.* Children draw a line from the girl to the correct picture (clean hands.) Finally, they color the girl and the clean hands.

**35**

# 👆 Point. 💬 Say. 📖 Match.

**Key Language:** *head, fingers, elbow, knee.* Children point to and name the body parts: *head, elbow, fingers, knee.* Then they look at the boy at the bottom of the page and draw lines to match the body parts at the top of the page to the corresponding parts on the boy's body. Finally, finger trace each line, repeating the name of the body part as you link the pictures (e.g. head – head).

# 🗨 Say.  ⬭ Trace.  ✏ Color.

**Key Language:** *I have two (ears / elbows / arms / knees).* Children look at the pictures. Point to the first picture, mime the action and say *I have two ears,* encouraging children to copy you. Then they follow the path with their finger. When they reach the next picture on the path, they mime the action and say the corresponding sentence: *I have two elbows. I have two arms. I have two knees.* Finally, children trace the path with a pencil or crayon and color the the body part indicated in each picture.

37

 Point. ✏ Color. 💬 Say.

**Key Language:** *blue, The (crayon) is blue.* **What color is the (book)? Is the (book) blue? Yes. / No.** Distribute crayons. Say: *Point to the crayon. The crayon is blue.* Children color the crayon blue. Repeat with the book. When they are finished coloring, ask: *What color is the (crayon)? Is the (book) blue?*

 Point. 🗨 Say. ✏ Color.

**Key Language:** *run, dance, crawl, kick.* Children point to and name the actions: *kick, dance, run, crawl.* Ask individual children: *Can you (dance)?* and encourage them to show you if they say *Yes.* Finally, children color the pictures of the actions they can do.

**39**

○ Trace. ■ Say.

**Key Language:** *S/he can (run). Can she (dance)? Yes, s/he can. No, s/he can't.* Point to the first child and ask: *Can he run? Can he dance? Can he kick?* Repeat as you point to each action. Finger trace the line from the boy to the action, then say: *He can (dance)!* Children trace the lines. Then, with your help, they say each action: *He can dance. She can run. He can kick (a ball).*

 Say. Make. Draw.

**Key Language:** *May I go to the bathroom? May I wash my hands? Yes, you may.* Remind children how we ask permission to go to the bathroom or wash our hands: *May I go to the bathroom? May I wash my hands?* Children repeat. Then children cover the palms of their hands with a light – colored paint and make a left and a right handprint on the page. Children can present their work, pointing and saying: *Dirty hands! Clean hands!* Finally, they use a brown crayon to draw dirt on the left handprint and blue and white crayons to draw water and soap on the right handprint.

 **Make.**

# My Fingerprints

**Key Language: *What can we do with our fingers? We can (paint).*** Say *Show me your fingers.* Children hold up their fingers and wiggle them in the air. Ask: *What can you do with your fingers?* Elicit answers, including *We can paint.* Then say: *We can make fingerprints!* and explain what it means. Children press each finger of their left hand onto an inkpad. Then they make fingerprints on the corresponding fingers of the left-hand outline. Monitor to ensure they make each fingerprint in the correct place. Repeat this procedure with the right hand.

◯ Trace. ¹²₃ Count. ✏ Color.

**Key Language:** *one, two, three, Show me (three). How many (children) can you see? Let's count.* Children say the *Number 3* chant as they show three fingers: *Three, three, show me three. Show me three like this.* Then they trace the number 3. Finally ask: *How many children can you see? Let's count: One, two, three.* Repeat, encouraging children to count. Finally, children color the three children as they repeat: *one, two, three.*

**43**

 Draw. Say.

# What can our bodies do?

**Key Language:** *arms, hands, legs, feet, head, fingers, elbow, knee, run, dance, crawl, kick, I have two (feet). I can (dance). I have two (legs). How many (legs) can you see?* Ask the Big Question: *What can our bodies do?* Children look back through Unit 3 of the Student's Book to recall what they have learned. Then they draw their favorite things from Unit 3 inside the frame. Ask volunteers to show their drawings to the class and name what they drew. Finally, answer the Big Question together, using the children's drawings to help.

# 4 What is a family?

 Point. 💬 Say. ✏️ Color.

**Key Language:** *father, mother, sister, brother.* Children point to and name the family members: *father, mother, sister, brother.* Then they color the picture. Finally, remind children that all families are different and allow volunteers to describe their family using the vocabulary words, e.g., *mother, brother, sister.*

■ **Say.** ○ **Circle.** ✎ **Color.**

# The Noisy House

**Key Language: *What can you see? Who's this? Where does the story take place? mother, father, sister, brother, grandfather, duck.*** Children look at the story scenes. Ask: *What can you see? Who's this? Where does the story take place?* Elicit answers using *I can see* / *This is...* Then ask: *Can you see the (mother)? Can you see a duck?* Children circle and then color the items in the pictures.

🔲 **Say.** ⭕ **Circle.** ✏️ **Color.**

**Key Language:** *What can you see? Who's this? Who are the characters?, night, lamb, duck, mother, father, sister, brother.* Children look at the story scenes. Ask: *What can you see?* Elicit answers using *I can see / this is...* Then ask: *Can you see night? Can you see a lamb / duck? Can you see a (sister)?* Children circle and color the items in the picture. Finally, children retell the story in their own words. Provide language as needed.

47

# 👁 Look. 💬 Say. ⭕ Trace.

**Key Language: Who's this? Who is in the story? Is this a character from the story?** Children look at the pictures of characters. Ask the questions: *Who's this? Who are the characters from the story?* encouraging children to answer (e.g. *Father.*). Then point to each one at a time and ask: *Is this a character from the story?* Children answer *Yes* or *No* and trace the circles around those characters who appear in the story.

# 👁 Look. 💬 Say. ✏️ Color.

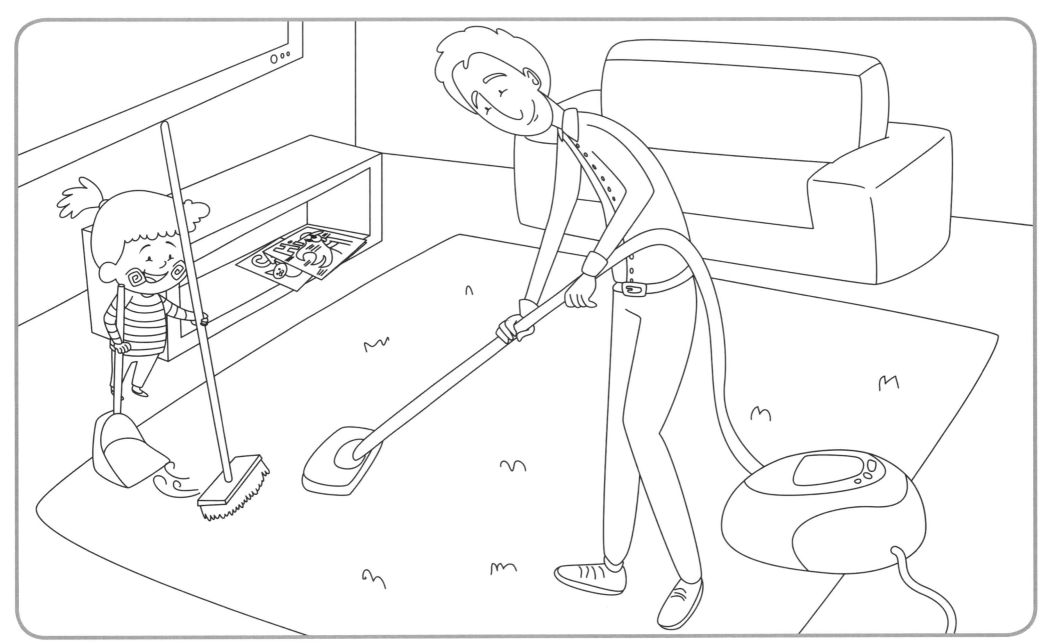

**Key Language: *How can we help our family? We can clean. We can help our mother / father*.** Children look at the scene and say what they see. Ask them what the girl is doing *(cleaning, helping her father)*. Ask: *How can we help our family?* and discuss the ways in which children help their family at home. Finally, children color the girl who is helping her family.

# 🔲 Say. ➡➡ Follow. ✏ Color.

**Key Language: *mother, baby, grandfather, grandmother*.** Point to the mother and ask children: *Who's this?* Demonstrate by finger tracing how to follow the path to the baby then point and say *Baby* as children repeat. Do the same for *grandfather* and *grandmother*. Then explain children should follow the paths between family members, drawing a path through the maze with a crayon and repeating their names. Finally, children color the family members.

**Glue.** **Color.** **Say.**

**Key Language:** *What is a family? Is he the (father)? Is she the (grandmother)? Yes, s/he is. No, s/he isn't. This is the (mother).* Have children bring a photograph of their family to class. They glue the photo in and then color the frame. As they are coloring, point and ask questions, such as: *Is (she) your (grandmother)?* encouraging children to answer *Yes, s/he is.* or *No, s/he isn't.* Finally, children share their photos with the class and describe their family members using *This is my* .... Encourage children to appreciate differences among the families.

👁 Look. 🗨 Say. ✏ Color.

**Key Language:** *yellow, blue, red, What color is the (mother) wearing? S/he is wearing yellow.* Children look at the family. Point to each and ask children to name them. Distribute crayons. Then ask: *What color is the mother wearing?* and answer *Yellow.* Children color the mother's clothes yellow. Continue with the grandmother, sister and brother, telling children what colors they are all wearing (blue, red, and yellow again).

# 🗨 Say. ✏ Color.

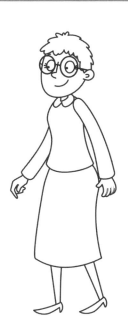

**Key Language: *young, old, short, tall*.** Point to the baby at the top left and ask: *Who's this? (A baby.)* Then ask: *Is the baby young or old? (Young.)* Explain to children they should find and color the family member on the right who is also young. Repeat with the grandfather and *tall / short*. Finally, children point to all the family members and say *young-old-young* and *tall-tall-short*.

👆 **Point.** 💬 **Say.** ✏️ **Color.**

**Key Language: *What does s/he look like? S/he's (short / tall / young /old)*.** Children look at the family members, point and name them together. Then say: *What do they look like?* Say: *He's short.* and children point to the boy. Continue with tall, old, and young, varying between male and female. Then ask children to describe the family members, modeling first, e.g., *The grandfather is old. He's tall.* Finally, distribute crayons. Say: *Color the short / young family members (yellow)!*

# 👁 Look. ✏ Color. 🔲 Say.

**Key Language:** *What's his/her name? His/Her name is (Kim / Dan / Mia / Leo).* Children look at the scene. Ask: *What can you see? Whose family is this?* (*Mia's / Leo's*). Say: *Color Mia and Leo's family.* Children color only the family members. Point to each family member and ask *What's her/his name?* encouraging children to answer using *His / Her name is ...* Finally, chidren practice asking the questions.

👁 **Look.** 🗨 **Say.** ⬭ **Trace.**

**Key Language:** *baby animals, This is the mother. This is the baby.* Look at the page together and ask: *Do animals have families? (Yes).* Point to the first animal and say *This is the mother. Help the mother find her baby.* Demonstrate by finger tracing how to trace the wavy line to the baby and say: *This is the baby!* Have children repeatedly finger trace the line saying *mother – baby!* Finally children trace with a crayon. Repeat for each mother-baby pair.

◯ Trace.  ₁³₂ Count.  ✏ Color.

**Key Language: *one, two, three, four, Show me (four). How many (babies) can you see? Let's count.*** Children say the *Number 4* chant as they show four fingers: *Four, four, show me four.* *Show me four like this.* Then children trace the number 4 several times with different colored crayons as they repeat: *Four, four, four.* Finally ask: *How many babies can you see? Let's count:* *one, two, three, four.* Repeat, encouraging children to count. Finally, children color the four babies as they repeat: *one, two, three, four.*

**57**

 **Draw.** **Say.**

# What is a family?

**Key Language:** *mother, father, sister, brother, grandfather, grandmother, baby, young, old, tall, short, This is my (mother). My (mother)'s name is … How many (fathers) can you see?* Ask the Big Question: *What is a family?* Children look back through Unit 4 of the Student's Book to recall what they have learned. Then they draw their favorite things from Unit 4 inside the frame. Ask volunteers to show their drawings to the class and name what they drew. Finally, answer the Big Question together, using the children's drawings to help.

# 5 What is a pet?

🔲 Say. ⬭ Trace. ✏️ Color.

**Key Language: *dog, bird, rabbit, fish.*** Children point to and name the pets: *dog, bird, rabbit, fish.* Then they trace around the animals, repeating the names. Finally, they color the animal they would like as a pet. Invite volunteers to tell you what they chose, asking: *What's your favorite pet?*

■ Say. ○ Circle. ✎ Color.

# Maisie's Pets

**Key Language:** *What can you see? Who are the characters? Where does the story take place? What's the story about? girl, cat, dog, window.* Children look at the story scenes. Ask the literacy questions. Elicit answers using *I can see* ... Then ask: *Can you see a (cat)?* Children circle and then color the items in the pictures.

# 🗨 Say. ○ Circle. ✏ Color.

**Key Language: *What can you see? Who are the characters? What's the story about?*, girl, cat, dog, window.** Children look at the story scenes. Ask the literacy questions. Elicit answers using *I can see ...* Then ask: *Can you see a window? Can you see Maisie?* Children circle and color the items in the picture. Then they retell the story in their own words. Provide language as needed.

61

**Say. Trace. Color.**

**Key Language:** ***Which characters are in the story? Is this a character from the story?*** Encourage children to point or reply with the pet names (*cat, dog*). Then point to each pet and ask: *Is this a character from the story?* If they say *Yes*, children trace a circle around the pet. Finally, children color the pets from the story.

👁 Look. 💬 Say. ✏ Color.

**Key Language:** *Take care of our pets. Help our pets. Feed our pets.* Children look at the scene and and say what they see. Ask them what the girl is doing *(Taking care of her pet fish. Feeding her pet fish)*. Ask: *How can we take care of our pets?* and discuss the ways in which children help their pets at home. Finally, children color the girl who is taking care of her pet.

63

 Point.  Say.  Color.

**Key Language: *turtle, cat, hamster, lizard.*** Children point to and name the pets: *turtle, cat, hamster, lizard.* Ask children: *What's your favorite pet?* Invite answers from all children. Finally, children color their favorite pet in the picture.

🗨 Say. 1²₃ Count. ✏ Color.

**1**

**2**

**3**

**Key Language: *How many (birds) can you see? I can see (three) (birds). Let's count.*** Say: *What number is this? (One.) How many turtles can you see? Let's count.* Count the one turtle with children and say: *I can see one turtle.* Children repeat. Then have them color the turtle. Continue in this manner with the remaining numbers and pets.

# 🗨 Say. ✏ Draw.

**Key Language:** *big, small, Is this (cat) big? Is this (dog) small?* Ask: *Is the cat big or small? (Big.)* Then say: *Let's draw a small cat!* and ask children to draw a small cat in the small empty box. Once they've finished, point to the small dog at the bottom of the page and ask: *Is the dog big or small? (Small.) Let's draw a big dog!* Ask children to draw a big dog in the big empty box. Finally, have children present their drawings and introduce them, e.g., *A small cat. A big dog.*

👆 **Point.** 💬 **Say.** 📖 **Match.**

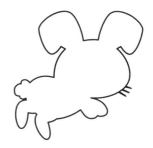

**Key Language:** *walk, jump, swim, fly.* Children point to the animals in the first column and name the actions: *swim, jump, walk, fly.* Then they draw lines to match the pets on the left with their outlines on the right. Finally, they finger trace the lines and say the actions as they link the illustrations, e.g., *swim – swim, jump – jump.*

# 👁 Look. 🗨 Say. ⭕ Circle.

**Key Language: *Can (cats) walk? Yes, they can. No, they can't. (Cats) can walk. (Cats) can't fly.*** Children look at each picture. Point to the dog and ask: *Can dogs fly?* Encourage answers using the language *No, they can't. / Yes, they can.* Then children use a green crayon to circle the pets who are running (hamster, dog). Finally, children say sentences about the animals: *Hamsters can run. Cats can walk. Fish can swim. Fish can't run.*

👆 **Point.** 💬 **Say.** ✏️ **Color.**

**Key Language:** *How do (pets) communicate? woof, meow, blub, chirp.* Explain you are going to make sounds different pets make and ask children to point to the correct pet. Say: *Woof, woof!* and children point to the dog. Continue with the other animal sounds and pets. Ask: *How do (dogs) communicate? (Woof, woof!)* encouraging children to make the animal sounds. Continue in this manner with the remaining pets. Then children color the pictures. Finally, children practice making the noises at different volumes.

👆 Point. 🔲 Say. ⭕ Circle.

**70**

**Key Language: *Is it a pet? Yes, it is. No, it isn't. It's a wild animal.*** Ask children to point to the animals in each row and guide them to name each of them *(dog, bear, lion, turtle, hamster, giraffe).* Then point to each and ask: *Is it a pet?* Encourage children to answer *Yes, it is.* or *No, it isn't.* Using a red crayon, children draw a circle around the animal that is not a pet in each row. Discuss wild animals and pets and how they are different.

◯ Trace. ₁²₃ Count. ✏ Color.

**Key Language: *one, two, three, four, five. Show me (five). How many (bubbles) can you see? Let's count.*** Children say the *Number 5* chant as they show five fingers: *Five, five, show me five. Show me five like this.* Then they trace the number 5. Finally ask: *How many bubbles can you see? Let's count: one, two, three, four, five.* Repeat, encouraging children to count. Finally, children color the five bubbles blue as they repeat: *one, two, three, four, five. (Blub, blub!)*

71

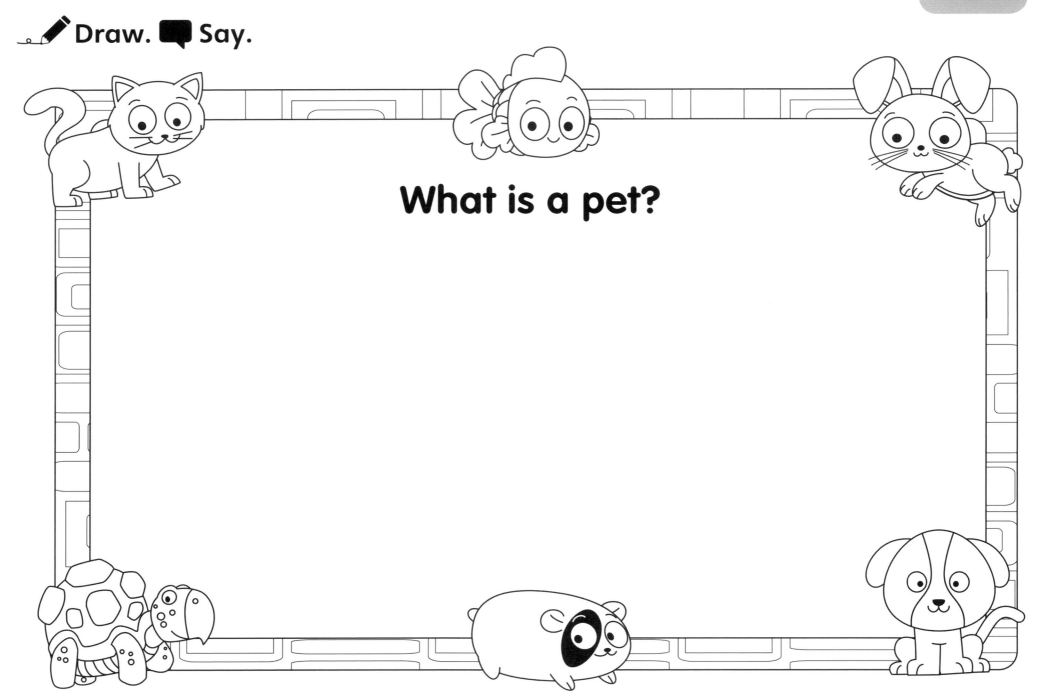

✏️ Draw. 💬 Say.

# What is a pet?

**Key Language:** *dog, bird, rabbit, fish, cat, turtle, hamster, lizard, big, small, How many (birds) can you see?, fly, walk, jump, swim, Can (birds) fly? Yes, they can. No, they can't. Birds can fly. Cats can't fly. How do (cats) communicate?, woof, meow, blub, chirp.* Ask the Big Question: *What is a pet?* Children look back through Unit 5 of the Student's Book to recall what they have learned. Then they draw their favorite things from Unit 5 inside the frame. Ask volunteers to show their drawings to the class and name what they drew. Finally, answer the Big Question together, using the children's drawings to help.

# 6 Can healthy foods be delicious?

🔲 Say. ⬭ Trace. ✏ Color.

**Key Language:** *apple, pear, tomato, carrot.* Children point to and name the fruits and vegetables: *apple, pear, tomato, carrot.* Then they trace the foods while repeating the name. Finally, they color the healthy foods.

**73**

 **Say.** ◯ **Circle.** ✏ **Color.**

# Healthy Hannah

**Key Language:** *What is the story about? What can you see? quail, pear, van, milk.* Children look at the story scenes. Ask the literacy questions. Elicit answers using *I can see ...* Then ask: *Can you see a van? Can you see milk?* Children circle and then color the items in the pictures.

■ Say. ○ Circle. ✏ Color.

**Key Language:** *What is the story about? What can you see?* ***healthy, pear, apple, carrot, quail.*** Children look at the story scenes. Ask the literacy questions. Elicit answers using *I can see ...* Then ask: *Can you see a pear? Can you see an apple? Can you see carrots? Can you see a quail?* Children circle and color the items in the picture. Finally, children retell the story in their own words. Provide language as needed.

75

👁 **Look.** ✏️ **Draw.** 💬 **Say.**

**Key Language: *Can you remember? Is this in the story?*, *carrots, fruit, apples, pears, milk.*** Ask children to think about the story. Ask: *Can you remember? What does Healthy Hannah like?* Point to each item and say: *Is this in the story?* Children draw lines from Healthy Hannah to the food she says she likes in the story. Finally, children name the items that Hannah eats: *carrots, fruit / apples and pears, milk.*

👁 **Look.** 💬 **Say.** ✏ **Color.**

**Key Language: *Wash fruit and vegetables. Eat healthy food.*** Children look at the scene. Ask children what foods Hannah says she eats in the story. *Does Hannah look happy? What foods is she going to eat? Are they healthy?* Finally, remind children why washing fruit and vegetables helps us stay healthy.

**77**

 Point. Say. Draw.

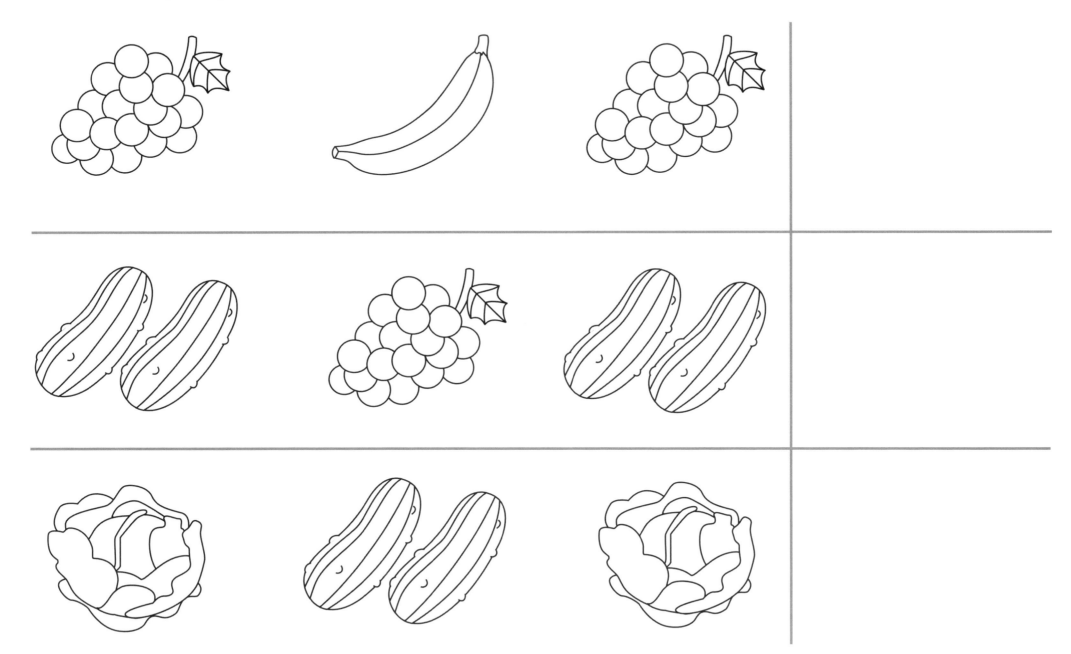

**78** **Key Language:** *bananas, grapes, cucumbers, lettuce.* Children point to and name the foods: *grapes, bananas, cucumbers, lettuce.* Then they look at the pattern in each row and say what food should come next. Guide them through the first pattern. Say: *grapes, banana, grapes. What comes next? (Banana.)* Children draw a banana in the empty space. Continue with the other rows. Once children have finished drawing, ask them to repeat the completed patterns, e.g., *grapes – banana – grapes – banana.*

# ✏ Draw. ✏ Color. ■ Say.

**Key Language: *Which (foods) do you like? I like (bananas).*** Children look at all the food items. Ask: *Which foods do you like?* Accept answers from some volunteers. Explain they can draw and color the child on the page to look like themselves and then color the food they like. Finally, children present their finished page and say which foods they like, e.g., *I like apples.*

79

🗨 Say. ◯ Trace. ✏ Color.

**Key Language: *circle, What shape is it? It's a circle. Trace the circles.*** Point to each food item and say: *What shape is it?* Finger trace a circle and say: *Circle.* Children copy you, finger tracing in the air and saying: *circle, circle, circle.* Then point to each item on the page and ask: *Is it a circle? (Yes. / No.)* Children trace the circles and color the tomatoes red.

👆 Point. ✏️ Color. 💬 Say.

**Key Language:** *pineapple, orange, potato, peas.* Children look at all the food items. Say: *Point to the (orange).* Distribute crayons of different colors and say: *Color the (orange).*
Repeat with the other items. Once they've finished coloring, children present their pages, pointing and naming the foods.

81

 **Draw.** **Color.** **Say.**

**Key Language: *What do you have ...? I have a/an ...*** Brainstorm all the food vocabulary children have learned in the unit *(tomato, apple, pear, carrot, grapes, banana, cucumber, lettuce, potato, pineapple, peas, orange)*. Children draw and color two food items in the lunchbox. Then they present their finished drawings and answer the question: *What do you have in your lunchbox?* using the structure *I have ...*

 **Draw.** ▌**Glue** 🗨 **Say.**

## What foods do you like?

**Key Language:** *I like (apples). Do you like (apples)? Yes, I do. No, I don't.* Ask children questions about various foods from the unit, encouraging them to answer with *Yes, I do.* or *No, I don't.* Explain they are going to draw themselves and make a picture of foods they like. Children add their face and hair to the blank face. Supply images or help children to cut out pictures of food they like from magazines. Children glue the pictures inside the thought bubble. Finally, they say what they like, e.g. *I like apples.* Provide any necessary language.

✏️ Draw. ✏️ Color. 💬 Say.

MILK

**Key Language: *sun, water, light (sunlight), soil, milk, What does it need? Does it need (sunlight)? It needs (water)*.** Point to the apple tree and ask children: *What does it need?* Point to each smaller picture and ask them, one at a time: *Does it need (sun)?* Children draw lines from the tree to the things it needs to grow. Finally, they color and practice saying, e.g., *It needs soil*.

# Trace. ¹²₃ Count. ✏ Color.

**Key Language:** *one, two, three, four, five, six. Show me (six). How many (dots) can you see? Let's count.* Children say the *Number 6* chant as they show six fingers: *Six, six, show me six. Show me six like this.* Then they trace the number 6. Have them follow the dots while they count and draw a line from 1 to 6 to complete the picture of the banana. Finally, children color the banana yellow.

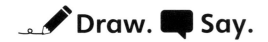 **Draw.** **Say.**

# Can healthy foods be delicious?

**Key Language:** *apple, pear, tomato, carrot, bananas, grapes, cucumbers, lettuce, pineapple, orange, potato, peas, circle, What do you like? I like (bananas). Do you like (apples)? Yes, I do. No, I don't. It's healthy. What do you have? I have ... How many (carrots) can you see?* Ask the Big Question: *Can healthy foods be delicious?* Children look back through Unit 6 of the Student's Book to recall what they have learned. Then they draw their favorite things from Unit 6 inside the frame. Ask volunteers to show their drawings to the class and name what they drew. Finally, answer the Big Question together, using the children's drawings to help.

# 7 What is a toy?

👆 Point. 💬 Say. 📖 Match.

**Key Language:** *car, teddy bear, doll, ball.* Children point to and name the toys at the top of the page. Then they draw a line to match the toys to their outlines in the toy box. Finally, they finger trace the lines and say the words as they link the illustrations: *ball – ball, doll – doll,* etc.

87

 **Say.** ○ **Circle.** ✏ **Color.**

# A Little Teddy Bear

**Key Language: *What can you see? What is the story about? teddy bear, yo-yo.*** Children look at the story scenes. Ask the literacy questions. Elicit answers using *I can see ...* Then ask: *Can you see a teddy bear? Can you see a yo-yo?* Children circle and then color the items in the pictures.

■ **Say.** ○ **Circle.** ✎ **Color.**

**Key Language: *What can you see? What is the story about? Where is teddy? Is it day or night? teddy bear, zipper.*** Children look at the story scenes. Ask the literacy questions. Elicit answers using *I can see / It is...* Then ask: *Can you see a teddy bear? Can you see a zipper?* Children circle and then color the items in the pictures. Finally, they retell the story in their own words. Provide language as needed.

👁 Look. ✏ Draw. ✏ Color.

**Key Language:** *Is this a scene from the story? Can you remember? Where is Teddy? Is it day or night? What happens next?* Point to the scene to the left of the page. Children draw a line from the first scene to the scene at the bottom right of the page. Then they color the teddy bear in the two where he's at home.

 **Look.** ■ **Say.** ✎ **Color.**

**Key Language: *sharing toys, Are they sharing the (toy)?*** Children look at the scene. Ask: *What are the children doing? (Playing with a toy car.) Are they sharing the toy? (Yes.)* Discuss why it is better to share toys so everyone is happy. Finally, children color the children who are sharing and the toy.

# 👆 Point. 💬 Say. 📖 Match.

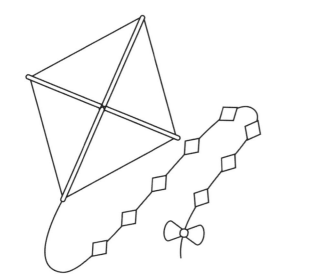

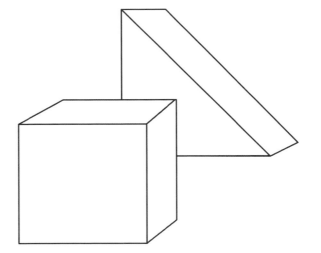

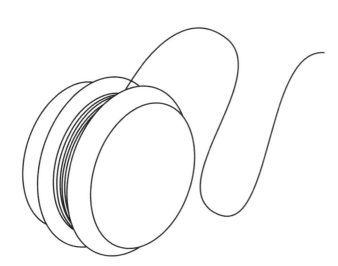

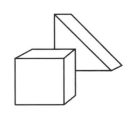

**Key Language:** *kite, tricycle, blocks, yo-yo.* Children point to and name the toys in the top row: *kite, tricycle, blocks, yo-yo.* Then they draw lines to match the corresponding big and small toys. Finally, children finger trace the lines and say the words as they link the illustrations, e.g., *big kite – small kite.*

✏️ Color. ⭕ Trace. 🔳 Say.

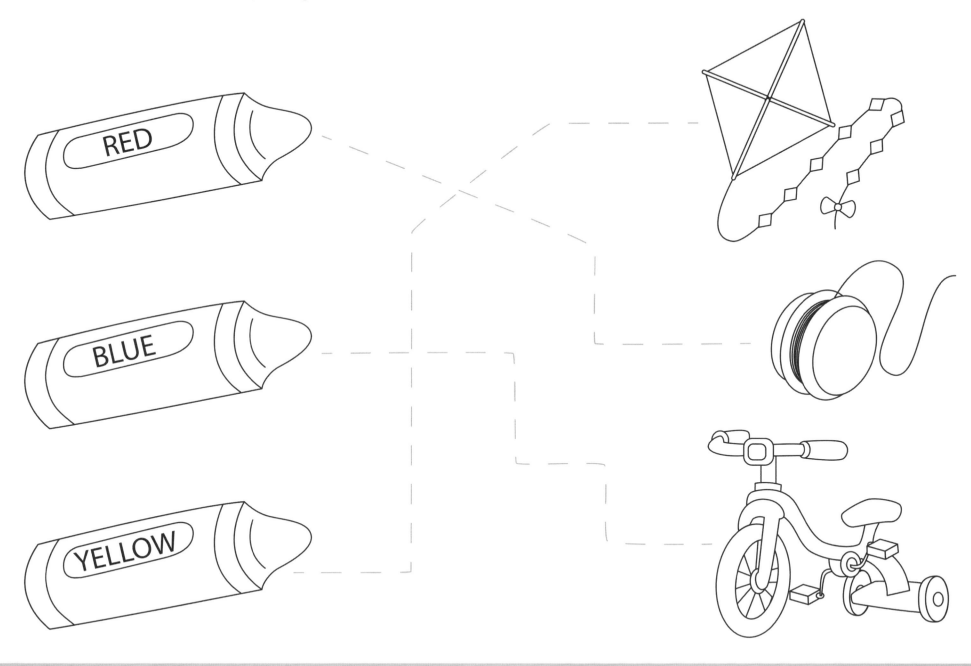

RED

BLUE

YELLOW

**Key Language:** *What color is the (ball)? The (ball) is (red). It's (red).* Have children color the first crayon red. Say: *The crayon is red.* Children repeat. Then they trace the line and color the yo-yo red. Repeat with the remaining colors and toys. Finally, ask: *What color is the kite / yo-yo / tricycle?* Encourage children to respond by saying *It's (yellow).* And *The (kite) is (yellow).*

93

# 👁 Look. 💬 Say. ✏ Color.

**Key Language: *What shape is it? It's a square.*** Children look at the scene. Ask what the girl is playing with *(blocks)*. Point to one of the square blocks at the bottom and say: *Look, it's a square.* Then point to each shape in the tower and ask: *Is it a square? (No.)* Explain that children should color only the squares. As they work, go around, point to a square and ask: *What shape is it?*

👆 Point. 💬 Say. ✏️ Color.

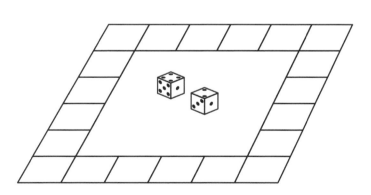

**Key Language:** *train, puzzle, board game, robot.* Children point to and name the items: *bird, train, robot, puzzle, rabbit, board game.* Ask: *What is a toy?* Children respond by pointing or by saying the name of one of the toys on the page. Point to each and ask: *Is it a toy?* Finally, they color only the toys.

👁 Look. ✏ Color. 🗨 Say.

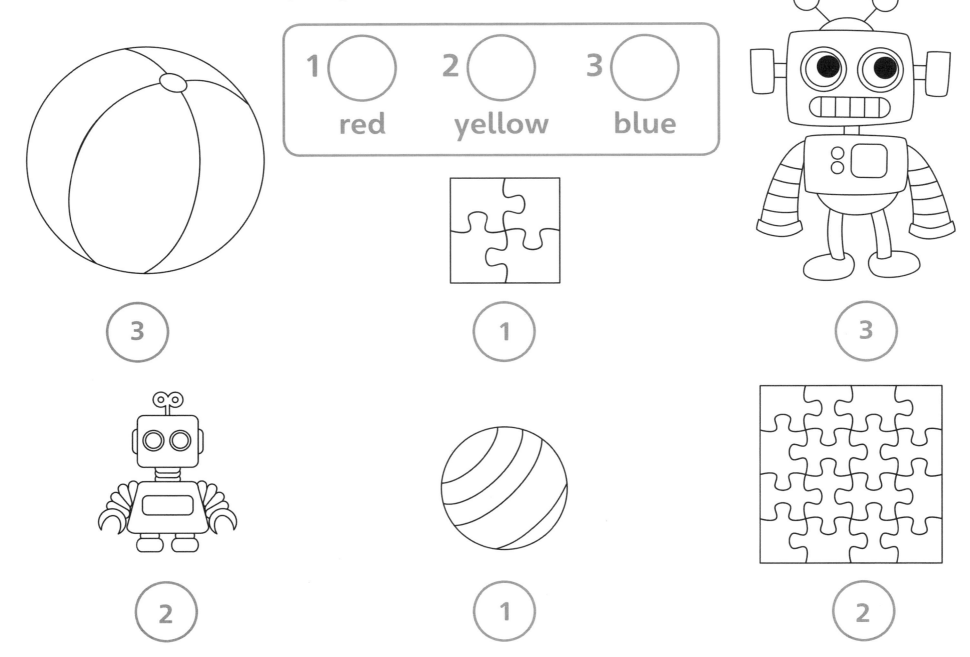

| 1 red | 2 yellow | 3 blue |

**Key Language:** *Is it big / small? Is it red / blue / yellow? Yes, it is. No, it isn't. The (ball) is (big) and (blue).* Explain to children they are going to color the toys 3 different colors. Distribute crayons, and tell them to color the circle beside number 1 red, circle 2 yellow, and circle 3 blue. Then have them color the toys using the color key as a guide. Finally, children say sentences about the toys, e.g., *The ball is big and yellow.*

 **Say.** **Draw.** **Color.**

**Key Language:** *I want a (teddy bear), please. Here you are. Thank you.* Ask: *Which toy do you want?* Allow children to respond, using the language *I want a (puzzle), please.* Children draw and color the toy they want inside the frame. Then ask volunteers to present their drawings, repeating, *I want a (doll), please.*

97

◯ Trace. 🗨 Say.

**Key Language:** *Match. half, parts.* Point to the picture and explain that half is missing and that children must draw the missing half to complete the picture. Discuss how each half is the same. Children trace the lines with pencil. When they've finished, ask: *What is it? (A teddy bear.)*

◯ Trace. ₁²₃ Count. ✏ Color.

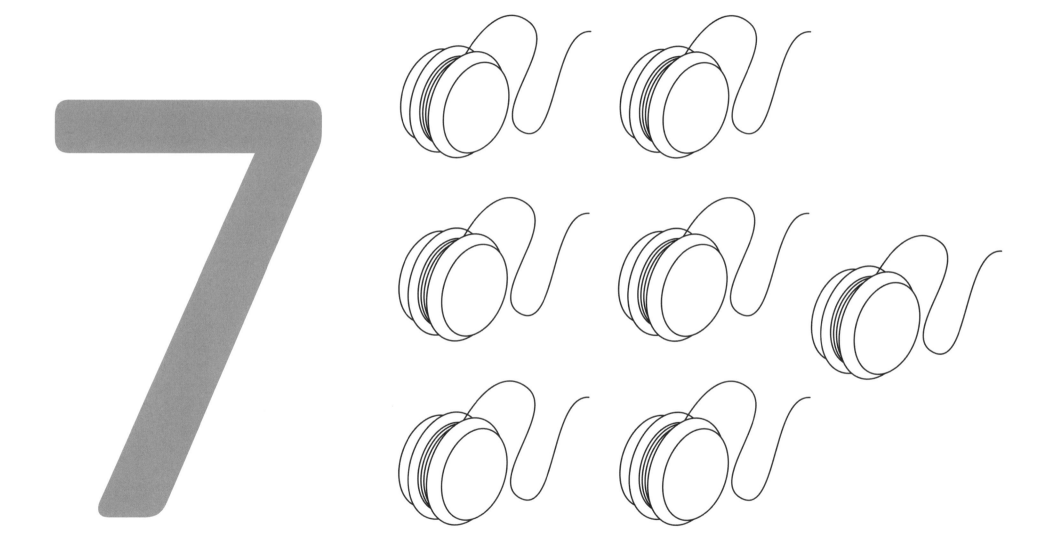

**Key Language: *one, two, three, four, five, six, seven. Show me (seven). How many (yo-yos) can you see? Let's count.*** Children say the *Number 7* chant as they show seven fingers: *Seven, seven, show me seven. Show me seven like this.* Then they trace the number 7. Ask: *How many yo-yos can you see? Let's count: One, two, three, four, five, six, seven.* Repeat, encouraging children to count. Finally, children color the seven yo-yos.

99

 **Draw.** **Say.**

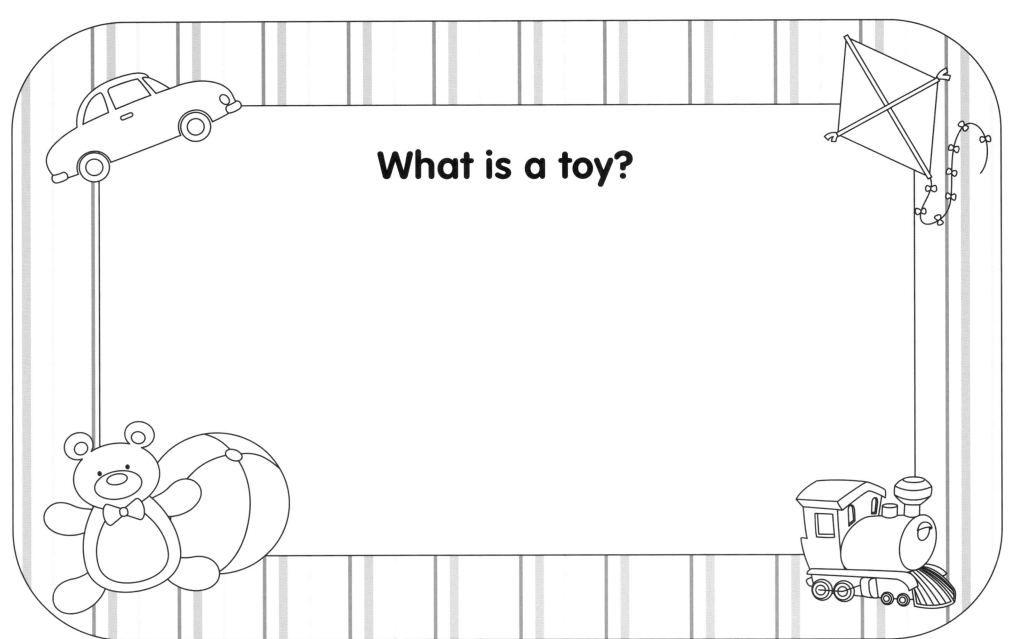

# What is a toy?

**Key Language:** *toys, teddy bear, doll, ball, car, yo-yo, kite, tricycle, blocks, puzzle, board game, train, robot, What color is the (ball)? It's (blue). Is it (small)? Yes, it is. No, it isn't. The ball is small and blue.* Ask the Big Question: *What is a toy?* Children look back through Unit 7 of the Student's Book to recall what they have learned. Then they draw their favorite things from Unit 7 inside the frame. Ask volunteers to show their drawings to the class and name what they drew. Finally, answer the Big Question together, using the children's drawings to help.

# (8) What can we see in a park?

👆 Point. 💬 Say. ✏️ Color.

**Key Language:** *tree, flower, grass, bee.* Children point to and name what they see: *tree, flower, grass, bee.* Then they color the picture.

■ **Say.** ○ **Circle.** ✎ **Color.**

Story

# Let's Play Together!

**Key Language:** *What can you see? What's the story about? Where does the story take place? Where is (my teddy bear)? It's (on the swing). teddy bear, iguana.* Children look at the story scenes. Ask the literacy questions. Elicit answers using *I can see ...* Then ask: *Can you see a teddy bear? Can you see an iguana?* Children circle and then color the items in the pictures.

# ■ Say. ○ Circle. ✏ Color.

**Key Language:** *What can you see? What's the story about? Where does the story take place? ant, umbrella.* Children look at the story scenes. Ask the literacy questions. Elicit answers using *I can see …* Then ask *Can you see an ant? Can you see an umbrella?* Children circle and then color the items in the pictures. Then they retell the story in their own words. Provide language as needed.

**103**

# 👁 Look. 📖 Match. 💬 Say.

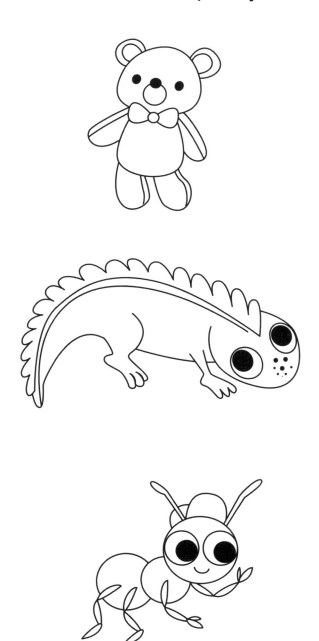

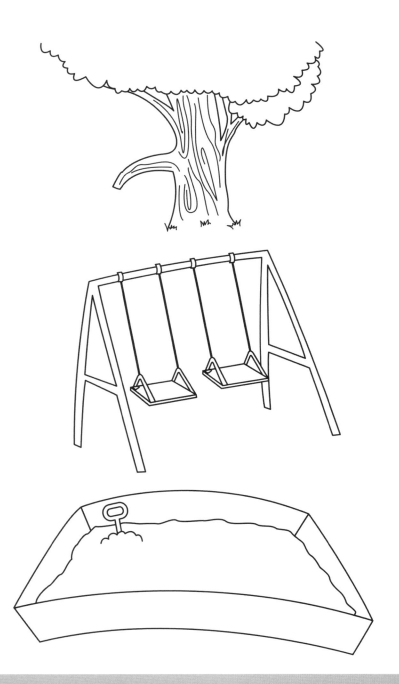

**Key Language: *What happens first / next / last?*** Children look at the toys and draw lines to match them to the place where they were hidden in the story. Then using the pictures on the left, moving top to bottom, re-tell the story together, prompting the children by asking: *What happens first? What happens next? What happens last?*

# 👁 Look. 💬 Say. ✏ Color.

**Key Language: *Keep our parks clean.*** Children look at the scene. Ask: *What are they doing? (Having a picnic in the park. Eating lunch. Cleaning up!). Are they keeping the park clean?*
*Who is keeping the park clean?* Discuss why it is important to keep our parks clean so they are beautiful and healthy for everyone to enjoy. Discuss what we can do to keep our parks clean (e.g., collect and throw garbage in the garbage can). Finally, children color the child who is keeping the park clean.

**105**

 Point. 💬 Say. ⚪ Trace.

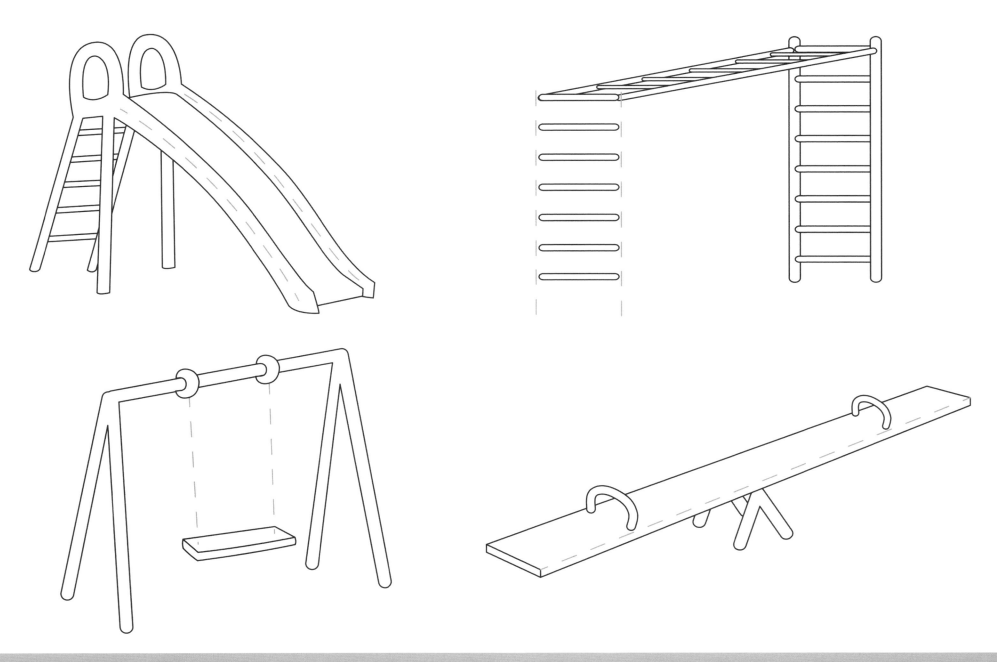

**Key Language:** *slide, swing, seesaw, monkey bars.* Children point to and name the the playground items. Then they trace the lines to complete the pictures, while repeating their names.

👁 Look. 💬 Say. 🖌 Paint .

**Key Language: *Do you like to play on the (swings)? Yes, I do. No, I don't.*** Point to each playground item and ask: *Do you like to play on the (seesaw)?* Encourage children to answer with *Yes, I do.* or *No, I don't.* Next they press their thumb onto an inkpad and make thumb prints on the items they like to play on, trying to place their prints in the location where they would play (for example, on top of the slide, on the seat of the swing, etc.)

**107**

👁 **Look.** ⭕ **Trace.** 🗨 **Say.**

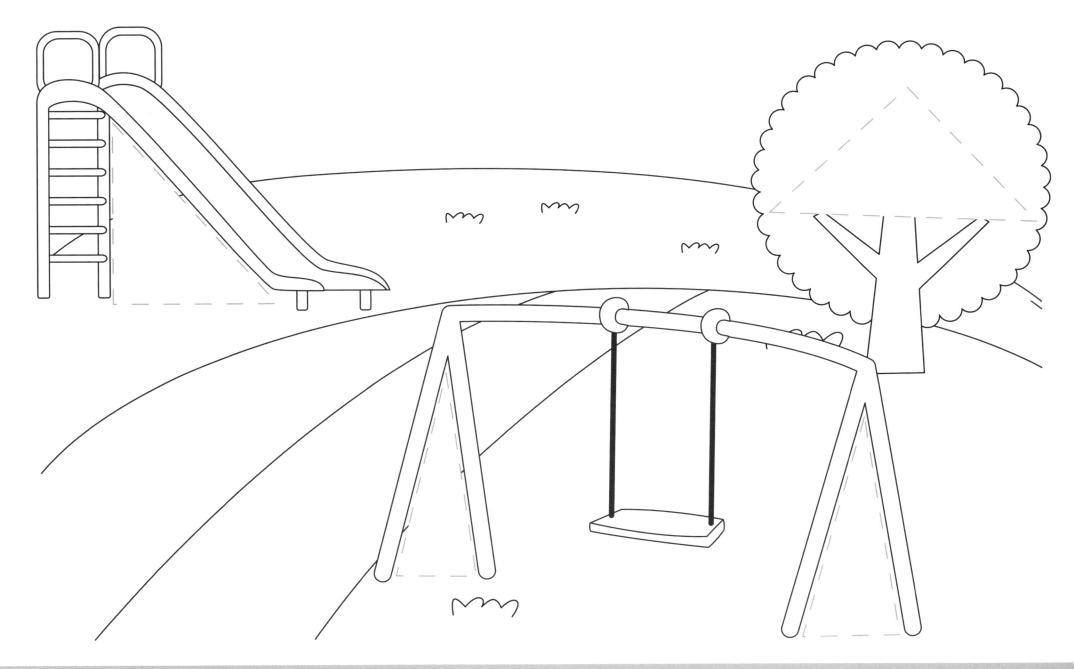

**Key Language: *triangle, What shape is it? It's a triangle.*** How many triangles can you see? Children look at the scene. Finger trace one of the triangles and ask: *What shape is it? (a triangle.)*
Repeat with the others. Children trace the triangles with crayons, repeating: *triangle, triangle, triangle.* Ask: *How many triangles can you see? (Four.)*

■ Say. ○ Circle. ✎ Color.

**Key Language:** *sun, cloud, sky, butterfly.* Point to the new vocabulary items and ask: *What's this?* Children name the items. Then children circle the sun, cloud and butterfly. Finally, they color the sky, sun, cloud and butterfly. As they're working, go around, point to the items and encourage children to repeat after you.

**109**

**Say.** **Trace.**

**Key Language: *What can you see? I can see a butterfly / some clouds.*** Point to items in the picture, asking: *What's this? (flower, swing, tree, cloud, etc.)* Then draw their attention to the tracing lines and explain children should complete the picture by tracing. When they're finished, ask: *What can you see?* Point out that there are multiple flowers, clouds and trees, but only a single bee, sun, swing and butterfly. Model *I can see some clouds. I can see a bee* and invite volunteers to use this language.

 Color. Say.

**Key Language:** *What color is it? Green; What does it look like? It's (big / small / red / yellow / blue / green).* Children point to and name the objects. Distribute red, blue, yellow and green crayons, holding each up and asking: *What color is it?* Children color the items as they like. Finally, children present their pages. Ask: *What does it look like?* Children describe using the language, e.g., *It's (yellow and red). It's small.* Finally, have children practice asking the questions.

**🗨 Say. ⭕ Circle. ✏ Color.**

**Key Language:** *What can you see in a park? Can you see a ...? Yes. No.* Children name the items on the page: *tree, butterfly, board game, hamster, flower, bird, seesaw.* Ask: *What can you see in the park?* Children circle the items they can see in the park (not the hamster or the board game). Then they color the picture, omitting the hamster and game.

◯ Trace.  ¹₃² Count.  ✏ Color.

**Key Language: one, two, three, four, five, six, seven, eight. Show me (eight). How many (suns) can you see? Let's count.** Children say the *Number 8* chant as they show eight fingers: *Eight, eight, show me eight. Show me eight like this.* Then they trace the number 8. Ask: *How many suns can you see? Let's count: one, two, three, four, five, six, seven, eight.* Repeat, encouraging children to count. Finally, children color the eight suns as they count to eight.

# ✏️ Draw. 💬 Say.

What can we see in a park?

**Key Language:** *tree, flower, grass, bee, slide, swing, seesaw, monkey bars, sun, cloud, sky, butterfly, green, red, blue, yellow, big, small, What can you see in a park? I can see a seesaw / some trees, Do you like to play on the swings? Yes, I do. No, I don't.* Ask the Big Question: *What can we see in a park?* Children look back through Unit 8 of the Student's Book to recall what they have learned. Then they draw their favorite things from Unit 8 inside the frame. Ask volunteers to show their drawings to the class and name what they drew. Finally, answer the Big Question together, using the children's drawings to help.

# 9 Where do we live?

 Point. Say. Draw.

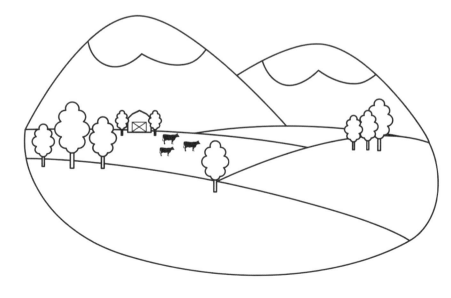

**Key Language:** *city, country, house, farm.* Children point to and name what they see: *farm, house, city, country.* Then they discuss where you can see a farm (in the country) and where you can see a house (in a town or a city) and draw a line to match the farm to the country scene and the house to the city scene. Discuss the fact that you can also see houses in the country, but you can't see a farm in the city! Finally, children color the scene that resembles the place where they live.

**■ Say. ○ Circle. ✏ Color.**

# There Is a Woman Who Lives in an Orange Shoe

**Key Language: *What can you see? Where does the story take place? What happens in the story? Can you remember? shoe, orange.*** Children look at the story scenes. Ask the literacy questions. Elicit answers using *I can see ...* Then ask: *Can you see a shoe? Can you remember the color of the shoe in the story? (Orange.)* Children circle the shoe in both images and color the pictures.

■ **Say.** ○ **Circle.** ✏ **Color.**

**Key Language:** *What can you see? Where does the story take place? What happens in the in the story? Where are they? orange, elephant.* Children look at the story scenes. Ask the literacy questions. Elicit answers. Then ask: *Can you see an elephant?* Children circle the elephant and color the scenes. Finally, children retell the story in their own words. Provide language as needed.

 Point. Say. Trace.

1

2

3

**Key Language:** *What happens first / next / last?* Children look at the scenes, point to each one, finger trace the line from one scene to the next, and say: *First, next, last.* Then they trace lines with a pencil. Point to the scenes and say: *One, two, three.* Children repeat and then trace the numbers. Explain how the numbers go in order, just like the scenes. Finally, point to the scenes in order and re-tell the story together.

👁 Look. 💬 Say. ✏ Color.

**Key Language:** *love, mother, children, family, How can we show we love someone?* Ask: *What can you see?* Elicit answers using *I can see ...* Then ask the value question: *How can we show we love someone?* Ask children to look at the scene and say: *What is the mother doing?* Discuss how the mother is showing she loves her child by spending time with and cooking for them. Children color the mother.

**119**

 **Point.** **Trace.** **Say.**

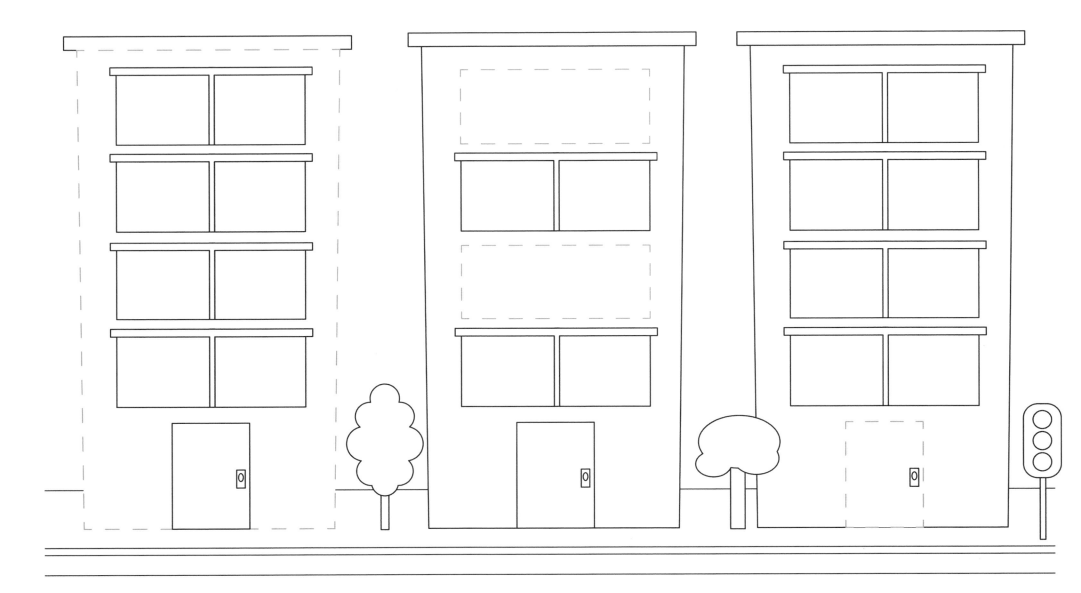

**Key Language:** *apartment building, window, door, street.* **Point to a (window).** Children look and point. Continue with the other vocabulary items, repeating each several times. Then say: *Trace a window / a door / an apartment building / the street* and have children trace the corresponding lines. Finally children finger trace around the objects and say the names.

 **Draw.** 💬 **Say.**

**Key Language: *Where do you live? I live in a house / an apartment building. Where does s/he live? S/he lives in a / an ...*** Ask: *Where do you live? A house or an apartment building?* Children answer. Distribute colored pencils or crayons and ask children to draw where they live. Then ask individual children: *Where do you live? (In an apartment building.)* Finally, summarize by saying: *(Sara) lives in a house. Where does (Ali) live?* and encourage children to respond as you go around the class.

**121**

👆 Point. ➤➤ Follow. 🗨 Say.

**Key Language:** *near, far, The (park) is far. The (house) is near.* Children look at the activity and find Mia. Then say: *Point to the house. The house is near. Point to the park. The park is far.* Children draw a very short line from Mia to the house saying *near, near, near* and a very long line, following the path, from Mia to the park, saying *far, far, far!*

👆 Point. 🗨 Say. ✏ Color.

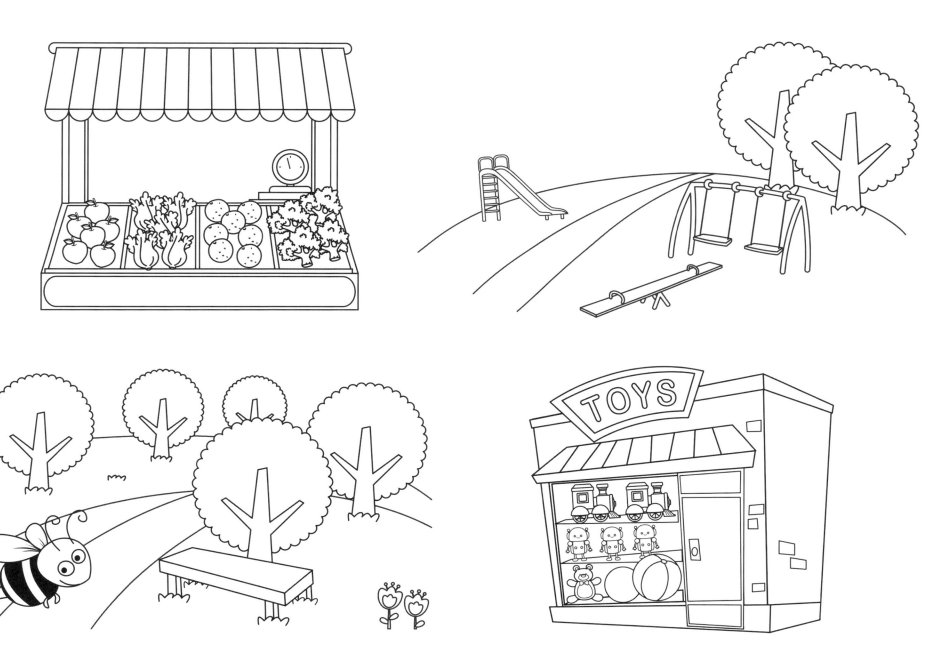

**Key Language: *park, playground, market, toy store*.** Children point to and name the places on the page: *market, playground, park, toy store*. Then ask: *Where can we see fruits and vegetables?* *(A market.)* Repeat with the remaining scenes: *Where can we see a swing and a slide?* *(A playground.)* *Where can we see trees and flowers?* *(A park.)* *Where can we see a teddy bear and a robot?* *(A toy store.)* Ask children: *Which is near your house?* Allow all to point and answer. Children color the place that is nearest to their house.

**123**

 Draw. Color. Say.

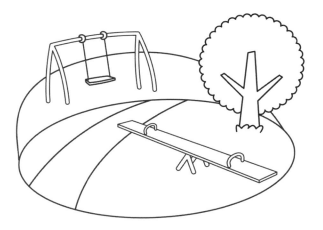

**Key Language:** *What can you see near your house? I can see a (park) near my house.* Children draw their home at the bottom left of the page. Then they draw lines from their home to the places they can see near their home. Finally, children color the places they can see from their home and answer the question: *What can you see near your house? (I can see a park near my house.)*

🔲 Say. ⭕ Trace.

**Key Language: *What do you want to do? I want to (play on the slide). Let's go to the (playground)!*** Look at the page together and ask children: *What do you want to do?* Elicit ideas and encourage answers using *I want to ... (run / play on the swings / kick a ball,* etc.). Say: *Let's go to the playground!* Children repeat. Demonstrate by finger tracing how to follow the path to the playground and then distribute crayons. Children follow the path with a crayon and color the playground when they arrive. Finally, children practice making suggestions.

**125**

 Draw. Say. Color.

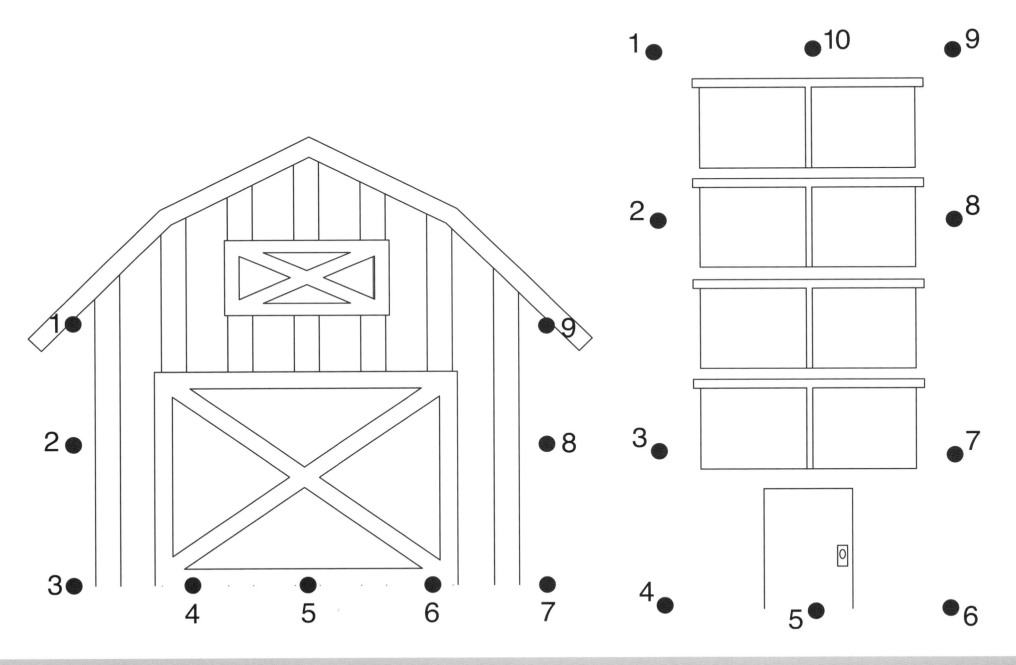

**Key Language: *Can you see a (farm) in the country? I can see an (apartment building) in the city.*** Children draw lines to connect the dots in the first picture, from 1 to 9. Demonstrate first by finger tracing, with children copying. Ask: *What is it? (It's a farm!) Can we see a farm in the city? (No.) Can we see farm in the country? (Yes.)* Repeat with the apartment building, connecting the dots, discovering the picture, and asking the questions. Finally, children color the farm and the apartment building.

○ Trace. ¹²₃ Count. ✏ Color.

**Key Language:** *one, two, three, four, five, six, seven, eight, nine, ten. Show me (nine / ten). How many (windows) can you see? Let's count.* Children say the *Number 9* chant as they show nine fingers: *Nine, nine, show me nine. Show me nine like this.* Then they trace the number 9. Point to the number 9 and say: *What number is this? (Nine.) Let's count: One, two, three, four, five, six, even, eight, nine. Nine mountains!.* Then they color the triangular mountains. Repeat this procedure with the number 10 and the windows.

127

 **Draw.** **Say.**

# Where do we live?

**Key Language:** *house, city, country, farm, street, apartment building, door, window, park, market, playground, toy store, I live in (a house). I can see a (park) near my house, near / far.*
Ask the Big Question: *Where do we live?* Children look back through Unit 9 of the Student's Book to recall what they have learned. Then they draw their favorite things from Unit 9 inside the frame.
Ask volunteers to show their drawings to the class and name what they drew. Finally, answer the Big Question together, using the children's drawings to help.

# Picture Dictionary

Children open the book to the corresponding unit. They point to a picture and name it. If children cannot name the vocabulary item, say the word and have them repeat it. Finally, children color the pictures.

129

| Unit 1 / Vocabulary 1 | Unit 1 / Vocabulary 2 | Unit 1 / Vocabulary 3 | Unit 2 / Vocabulary 1 |
|---|---|---|---|
| teacher | book | Leo | face |
| boy | crayon | Mia | hair |
| girl | table | Tickles | eyes |
| school | chair | | nose |

| Unit 2 / Vocabulary 2 | Unit 2 / Vocabulary 3 | Unit 3 / Vocabulary 1 | Unit 3 / Vocabulary 2 |
|---|---|---|---|
| forehead | sad | arms | head |
| mouth | happy | hands | elbow |
| ears | angry | legs | fingers |
| cheecks | | feet | knee |

| Unit 3 / Vocabulary 3 | Unit 4 / Vocabulary 1 | Unit 4 / Vocabulary 2 | Unit 4 / Vocabulary 3 |
|---|---|---|---|
| run | father | baby | young |
| dance | mother | grandfather | old |
| crawl | sister | grandmother | tall |
| kick | brother | | short |

| Unit 5 / Vocabulary 1 | Unit 5 / Vocabulary 2 | Unit 5 / Vocabulary 3 | Unit 6 / Vocabulary 1 |
|---|---|---|---|
| dog | turtle | swim | apple |
| bird | cat | jump | pear |
| fish | hamster | walk | tomato |
| rabbit | lizard | fly | carrot |

| Unit 6 / Vocabulary 2 | Unit 6 / Vocabulary 3 | Unit 7 / Vocabulary 1 | Unit 7 / Vocabulary 2 |
|---|---|---|---|
| grapes | pineapple | teddy bear | kite |
| bananas | orange | ball | tricycle |
| cucumber | potato | car | blocks |
| lettuce | peas | doll | yo-yo |

| Unit 7 / Vocabulary 3 | Unit 8 / Vocabulary 1 | Unit 8 / Vocabulary 2 | Unit 8 / Vocabulary 3 |
|---|---|---|---|
| train | tree | slide | sun |
| robot | flower | monkey bars | cloud |
| puzzle | grass | swing | sky |
| board game | bee | seesaw | butterfly |

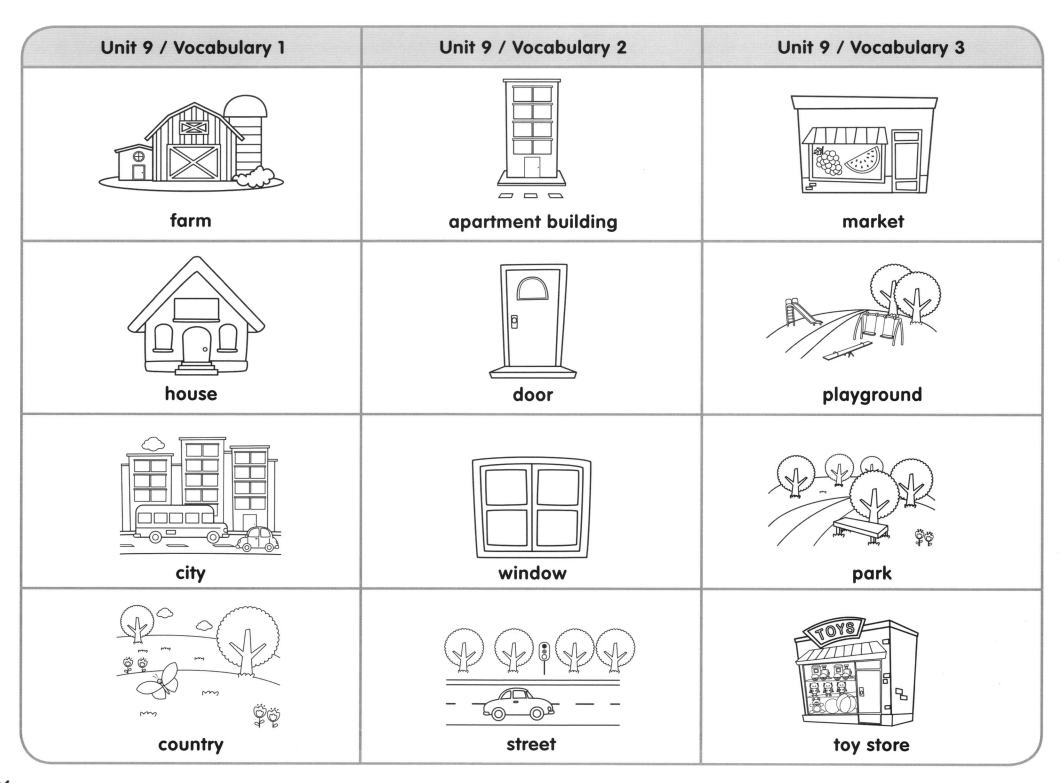

| Unit 9 / Vocabulary 1 | Unit 9 / Vocabulary 2 | Unit 9 / Vocabulary 3 |
|---|---|---|
| farm | apartment building | market |
| house | door | playground |
| city | window | park |
| country | street | toy store |

136